WHEN THE gROUND SHAKES

Workbook

CHILDREN 911 RESOURCES
EMPOWERING PARENTS FOR CHILDREN

This Workbook is dedicated to all children
who live in earthquake-prone areas.

AUTHORS   Irit Almog & Shoshana Wheeler

ILLUSTRATOR   David R. Aseraf

DESIGNER   Yael Michelson

EDITOR   Sharone Almog

www.children911resources.com
Children911Resources@gmail.com

Children 911 Resources
5308 Derry Avenue
Suite L 201
Agoura Hills CA 91301

This workbook belongs to:

....

Introduction

Children learn about the world from their parents, teachers, and caregivers. It is through adult actions and examples that we teach them how to react to various circumstances in life. In order to best help our children, we need to understand the range of reactions they may have to certain traumas and events, and how to best cope with those responses. During a crisis or disaster, children will all experience different emotional reactions, ranging from minor to severe. Our mission and hope is that through these activities you will gain an understanding of how a child may feel in a crisis or catastrophic event. Through this empathetic process, you will learn how to help your child/student best cope under stressful circumstances.

Young children may not know the specific words they need to use in order to express their fears and anxieties. Our activities provide outlets for such children to express their thoughts in a more creative and productive manner.

In the event of a crisis we want YOU to be the child's emotional coach. We want to empower you so that you can provide guidance to children with our tools. It is very important to practice these games and exercises, as repetition is fundamental to learning. For example, through daily practice of learning letters and sounds, children learn to read and write. We hope you have fun practicing these activities, so that in the event of a crisis, your child/student will be prepared and know how to respond. It is equally as important to practice and play these activities after a crisis occurs in order to help them process the experience.

Letter to helper,

Dear Teachers, Parents, and Caregivers:
In the event of an unpredictable situation such as an earthquake, tornado, hurricane, or flood, this workbook will provide children with the tools they need in order to cope with their feelings. Specifically designed to prepare children for a natural disaster, this workbook was created to reduce their stress and anxiety levels before, during, and after the event. We are excited for this workbook to benefit both you and your children in the event of an unforeseen disaster.

Warmly,
Irit Almog (MA, LMFT) & Shoshana Wheeler (MA)

5

A lot of things can **move** and **shake**.

Circle the items that can move and shake. Color them in.

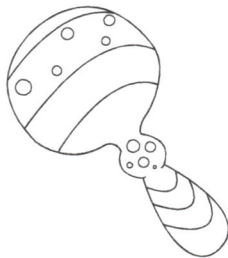

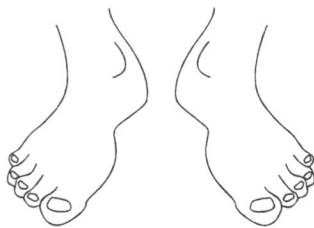

6

Note to Helper: On this page we are introducing the idea that some things are intended to shake like hands, feet and salt shakers. Other things shake unintentionally. This page instructs the child to circle things that shake intentionally.

Draw or write something else
that can move or shake.

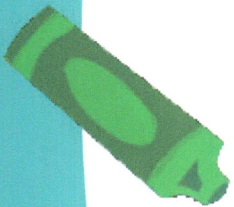

Draw a picture of yourself moving and shaking.

Draw or write something else
that can move or **shake**.

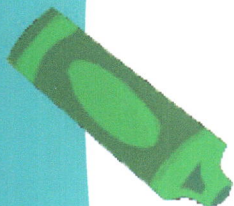

7

Draw a picture of yourself moving and **shaking**.

8

Earthquakes are always a surprise. We don't know when they are going to occur. Color all of the surprised faces.

Draw a picture of a time when you were surprised.
What happened?

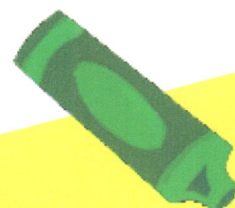

10 *

Earthquakes happen deep under the ground where we can't see.

What else is underground that we can't see? Color them in.

Note to Helper: The intent of this activity is for the child to become aware that things occur underground that we can't see, just like an earthquake.
If you or the child comes up with more examples, add them to the page.

Draw a line from the picture on the left to how it makes you feel on the right.

13

Loud noises can be scary. Movies can be scary.
When the earth moves, it can also be scary.
Draw a time you felt scared.

Show the best place to go during an earthquake.
Draw a line to match the pairs.

Note to helper: Here we are introducing other areas that aren't address in the earthquake book. Please take this opportunity to teach what to do in other situations that aren't listed that you believe your child may encounter. In the stadium/theatre- stay in your seat. If you are outside - move Towards open areas, away from high buildings & glass

15

When the earth shakes, it usually lasts about 15 seconds. Color in the numbers. When you are done, take three deep breaths, and count to 15 slowly. How do you feel? Share your feelings with an adult.

1 2 3 4 5
6 7 8 9
10 11 12
13 14 15

Note to helper: It is important for the child to know that when an earthquake occurs it is time limited. Having something to do during an earthquake, such as counting, helps reduce anxiety and fear. It is important to repeat the relaxation and breathing techniques as often as possible. This will help the child master the skill so they know what to do when faced with a fearful situation.

Some earthquakes may last more than 15 seconds. If you counted to 15 and the earth is still shaking, start singing your favorite songs. With your helper, make a list of your 3 favorite songs & practice singing them together.

1.

2.

3.

16

When you hear the word earthquake, how does it make you feel?

Close your eyes and imagine the feeling in your body...

Color your feeling on the body & then talk to your helper about your feelings.

Write or draw the things that make you happy.

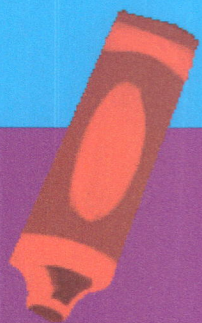

18

Think about safe spots in each room of your house. For example: under a desk, under a table, or against an inside wall. Draw your safe place in each room of your home.

21

Living room:

Kitchen:

Your room:

Note to helper: Add any other rooms that you have in your home.

Here are some ideas that can help reduce your fear:

1. Take a deep breath. Hold it to the count of 3. Release it to the count of 5. Repeat for 3 breaths.

2. Squeeze your muscles and then **relax them**

3. Choose a color and ll the page - scribble all over.

4. Scrunch your face and relax - repeat this **3** times.

5. Sing your favorite song.

20

6. Give your parents a big hug, and then give yourself a **big hug**.

The Power of Positive Thinking

This activity will help take away any negative feelings you may be having and will replace them with new, more positive emotions. If you have been feeling scared, sad, anxious, or any other bad feeling, this activity will help you feel more calm and relaxed. Practice this activity as needed with as many emotions as you are feeling. You can draw pictures or write down answers.

21

What do you love? (this might be a pet, a toy, or a person, etc.)

What is one thing you love about it?

What else do you love about it?

What is another thing you love?

What do you love about it?

What else do you love about that?

Note to helper: This simple activity draws your child's attention away from the overwhelming emotions they may be feeling and helps calm them into a state of regulation. When you child has been angry, sad, or anxious for a while, you can tell them that this practice will help them feel better. This empowers the child and helps guide them into a more positive state of being. It gives them a break from the negative emotion they might be feeling (such as fear, sadness, or anxiety) and helps change their state of mind.

Practice this activity as needed with as many emotions as you see fit.

On this page draw how you felt during the event and how you are feeling now.

How did you feel during the event?

How are you feeling now?

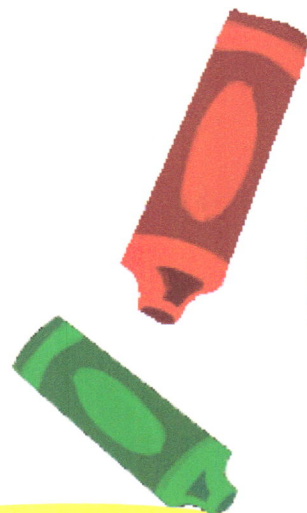

22

Making Sense of What Happened
When The Ground Shakes

Things I can do to meet my needs?

What were my thoughts

When The Ground Shakes What Happened

What do I need; What's important to me

How did I feel?

1.

2.

3.

Finger Holds

Finger holds are a great way to calm down from an emotional state. Each finger is correlated to a specific emotion.

The ring finger is for anxiety or nervousness

The middle finger is for anger and rage.

The index finger is for fear

The pinky finger is for self-esteem or when feeling the victim of a circumstance

The thumb is for grief, tears, and emotional pain

24

Note to Helper: Ask the child how they are feeling, and then hold their corresponding finger that matches their state of being. Once you hold their finger, tell them to take a deep breath in and imagine they are letting in feelings of peace and calmness. Upon exhaling, tell them to imagine they are breathing out the emotion they want to release and get rid of. Do this several times. Your child will soon feel better, calmer, and relaxed.

EXAMPLE: If your child is feeling scared, you or the child can hold their index finger. Wrap your hand around the finger, holding it snugly in your fist. Instruct the child to breathe in deeply and imagine they are breathing in calmness and peace. On the exhale, instruct your child to breathe out the fear. Repeat several times until the child is feeling calmer.

Choose a puppet to color. Cut and glue it to the stick. Have the puppet tell where to go and what to do during an earthquake. Note to Helper: You can also use the puppet to read the book.

Help the child cut and glue the two faces back to back to the paper stick below. Talk about or role play different situations and ask the child to hold up the face that matches how they think they would feel in the situation.
Add to the situations: How would you feel if you heard the word earthquake? How do you feel knowing that earthquakes always end?

26

Drawing My Feelings

27

Earthquake Kit for Kids

Ten Essential items in the event of an earthquake:

1. Whistle
2. Flashlight
3. Water
4. Energy Bar
5. Baggie with band-aids
6. Glasses (if you wear them)
7. Your favorite toy or stued animal
8. Crayons or markers
9. Change of clothes
10. "When The Ground Shakes" workbook

Parents, this emergency kit is for your child.

If there is something pertaining to him/her that you think he/she should have, please add it to the list.

For a detailed family Earthquake Preparedness Kit, go online to:

www.FEMA.gov/disaster.

www.ingramcontent.com/pod-product-compliance
Lightning Source LLC
Chambersburg PA
CBHW060816090426
42737CB00002B/83